Teachers' Day

Thank You

It is Teachers' Day.

We say thank you
to our teacher.

Look at the flowers.

The flowers
are for my teacher.

Look at the card.

The card

is for my teacher too!

My brother
will say thank you
to his teacher.

My sister
will say thank you
to her teacher.

13

We will all

say thank you

to our teachers.

Thank you!